~A BINGO BOOK~

Kansas
Bingo Book

COMPLETE BINGO GAME IN A BOOK

Written By Rebecca Stark

ISBN 978-0-87386-509-8

Educational Books 'n' Bingo

Printed in the U.S.A.

DIRECTIONS

INCLUDED:

List of Terms

Templates for Additional Terms and Clues

2 Clues per Term

30 Unique Bingo Cards

Markers

1. **Either cut apart the book or make copies of ALL the sheets. You might want to make an extra copy of the clue sheets to use for introduction and review. Keep the sheets in an envelope for easy reuse.**

2. Cut apart the call cards with terms and clues.

3. Pass out one bingo card per student. There are enough for a class of 30.

4. Pass out markers. You may cut apart the markers included in this book or use any other small items of your choice.

5. Decide whether or not you will require the entire card to be filled. Requiring the entire card to be filled provides a better review. However, if you have a short time to fill, you may prefer to have them do the just the border or some other format. Tell the class before you begin what is required.

6. There are 50 terms. Read the list before you begin. If there are any terms that have not been covered in class, you may want to read to the students the term and clues before you begin.

7. There is a blank space in the middle of each card. You can instruct the students to use it as a free space or you can write in answers to cover terms not included. Of course, in this case you would create your own clues. (Templates provided.)

8. Shuffle the cards and place them in a pile. Two or three clues are provided for each term. If you plan to play the game with the same group more than once, you might want to choose a different clue for each game. If not, you may choose to use more than one clue.

9. Be sure to keep the cards you have used for the present game in a separate pile. When a student calls, "Bingo," he or she will have to verify that the correct answers are on his or her card AND that the markers were placed in response to the proper questions. Pull out the cards that are on the student's card keeping them in the order they were used in the game. Read each clue as it was given and ask the student to identify the correct answer from his or her card.

10. If the student has the correct answers on the card AND has shown that they were marked in response to the *correct questions,* then that student is the winner and the game is over. If the student does not have the correct answers on the card OR he or she marked the answers in response to *the wrong questions,* then the game continues until there is a proper winner.

11. If you want to play again, reshuffle the cards and begin again.

Have fun!

TERMS INCLUDED

Abilene

Agricultural

Border

Buffalo

Chisholm Trail

Cottonwood(s)

County (-ies)

Dissected Till Plains

Dodge City

Amelia Mary Earhart

Earth Lodge(s)

Dwight D. Eisenhower

Executive Branch

Firefighter's Museum

Flag

Harney Silt Loam

Hard Chief's Village

High Plains

Honeybee

Indian Removal Act

Judicial Branch

Kansas City

Kansas–Nebraska Act

Leavenworth

Legislature

Lewis and Clark

Little Bluestem

Little Raven

Louisiana Purchase

Meadowlark

Mined

Mission(s)

Missouri River

Motto

Mount Sunflower

Pawnee(s)

River(s)

Salamander

Santa Fe Trail

Seal

Song

Southeastern Plains

Sunflower(s)

Topeka

Tornado (-oes)

Turtle

Tuttle Creek

Union

Wheat

Wichita

Additional Terms

Choose as many additional terms as you would like and write them in the squares. Repeat each as desired.
Cut out the squares and randomly distribute them to the class.
Instruct the students to place their square on the center space of their card.

Clues for Additional Terms

Write three clues for each of your additional terms.

_____ 1. 2. 3.	_____ 1. 2. 3.
_____ 1. 2. 3.	_____ 1. 2. 3.
_____ 1. 2. 3.	_____ 1. 2. 3.

KANSAS KANSAS KANSAS KANSAS KANSAS

KANSAS KANSAS KANSAS KANSAS KANSAS

KANSAS KANSAS KANSAS KANSAS KANSAS

KANSAS KANSAS KANSAS KANSAS KANSAS

KANSAS KANSAS KANSAS KANSAS KANSAS

KANSAS KANSAS KANSAS KANSAS KANSAS

KANSAS KANSAS KANSAS KANSAS KANSAS

Abilene

1. ___ began as a stagecoach stop in 1857. It grew when Joseph G. McCoy decided to locate his stockyards here.
2. The Eisenhower Presidential Library & Museum is located here.

Agricultural

1. Kansas is an important ___ state. Cattle, wheat, corn, and soybeans are the most important ___ products.
2. By far the highest ___revenue in Kansas comes from raising cattle and calves.

Border

1. These states ___ Kansas: Nebraska, Oklahoma, Missouri, and Colorado.
2. The Missouri River flows along the northeast ___ between Kansas and Missouri.

Buffalo

1. The American ___ is the state animal. The male can weigh over 1,800 pounds.
2. ___ once roamed the prairie by the tens of millions.

Chisholm Trail

1. The ___ was used in the late 19th century to drive cattle overland from ranches in Texas to Kansas railheads.
2. Wichita's location on the ___ made it a destination for cattle drives heading north to access railroads to the East.

Cottonwood(s)

1. The ___ is the state tree.
2. Pioneers staking out a new life on the prairie often planted these fast-growing trees to provide shade, warmth and cooking fuel.

County (-ies)

1. Kansas is divided into 105 ___.
2. Butler is the largest ___ in Kansas in area.
According to the 2010 Census, Johnson ___ was the most populous.

Dissected Till Plains

1. The ___ are in the northeastern part of the state. Rivers and streams have cut through, or dissected, the landscape, creating high bluffs.
2. The ___ can be roughly defined as the region north of the Kansas River and east of the Big Blue River.

Dodge City

1. In the 1800s, ___ became the largest cattle market in the world.
2. Named after the nearby fort, ___ is famous as a wild frontier town of the Old West.

Amelia Mary Earhart

1. This aviator was born in Atchison, Kansas. She was the first woman to fly solo across the Atlantic Ocean.
2. She disappeared in 1937 during an attempt to circumnavigate the globe.

Earth Lodge(s) 1. The ____ was once the main type of dwelling for Native Americans of the Central and Northern Great Plains. 2. ____ were circular, dome-shaped dwellings with a heavy timbered framework. They were covered with layers of branches, grass, and earth.	**Dwight D. Eisenhower** 1. This 5-star general and 34th President of the United States was raised in Abilene. 2. The boyhood home of this President is in Abilene.
Executive Branch 1. The ____ comprises the governor, the lieutenant governor, the secretary of state, and the attorney general. 2. The governor is head of the ____. The present-day governor is [fill in].	**Firefighter's Museum** 1. The Kansas ____ in Wichita is the restored historic Engine House No. 6. 2. The Kansas ____ is the restored site of the last horse-drawn fire station in Wichita.
Flag 1. The state ____ displays the Great Seal centered on a blue field. 2. Above the seal on the state ____ is the state crest; it depicts a sunflower resting on a twisted blue and gold bar. Below the seal is the name of the state in gold.	**Harney Silt Loam** 1. ____ is the state soil. It was chosen because it is an ideal prairie soil. 2. ____ is prime farmland, meaning it has the best combination of physical and chemical characteristics for producing food and fiber.
Hard Chief's Village 1. ____ provides a better understanding of the Kansa people of the 1800s. 2. This earthlodge village site in Shawnee County was occupied by Kansa Indians during the early Historic Period.	**High Plains** 1. The ____ form the western half of Kansas and are characterized by a gently rolling landscape. 2. The ____ have a higher elevation than the Southeastern Plains.
Honeybee 1. The ____ is the state insect. 2. The ____ is an official state symbol in 17 states, probably because it plays such an important role in agriculture. Kansas Bingo	**Indian Removal Act** 1. The ____ was signed into law by President Andrew Jackson on May 28, 1830. 2. The ____ called for the removal of Native Americans to federal territory west of the Mississippi River in exchange for their homelands. © **Barbara M. Peller**

Judicial Branch

1. The ___ interprets what our laws mean and makes decisions about the laws and those who break them.
2. The ___ is made up of several courts, the highest of which is the state Supreme Court.

Kansas City

1. ___ is part of a consolidated city-county government known as the Unified Government of Wyandotte County and ___.
2. ___ is situated at Kaw Point, which is where the Missouri and Kansas rivers meet. It is often called KCK to distinguish it from the city in Missouri.

Kansas–Nebraska Act

1. The ___ of 1854 created the territories of Kansas and Nebraska. It let the settlers of the two territories decide whether or not to allow slavery.
2. The ___ served to repeal the Missouri Compromise of 1820, which prohibited slavery north of latitude 36°30´.

Leavenworth

1. The federal prison at ___ was the largest maximum-security federal prison for male inmates in the United States from 1903 until 2005.
2. In 2005 the federal prison at ___ was downgraded to medium security.

Legislature

1. The ___ makes the laws.
2. The Kansas ___ consists of a 125-member House of Representatives and a 40-member Senate.

Lewis and Clark

1. The purpose of the ___Expedition, also known as the Corps of Discovery, was to explore the vast unknown territory west of the Mississippi River.
2. The ___ Expedition spent about 2 weeks exploring the northeast corner of what is now the state of Kansas.

Little Bluestem

1. ___ is the state grass.
2. ___ was once the most abundant grass in the Great Plains.

Little Raven

1. This Arapaho leader helped bring peace between warring Plains Indian tribes.
2. Because of his influence, the Southern Arapaho remained neutral during the Red River War of 1874–75.

Louisiana Purchase

1. Most of present-day Kansas came to the United States as part of this the ___.
2. The ___ of 1803 doubled the size of the United States and opened up the continent to its westward expansion.

Meadowlark

1. The western ___ is the state bird. It is in the same family as blackbirds and orioles.
2. The western ___ is a familiar songbird across the western two-thirds of the United States.

Kansas Bingo

Mined 1. Petroleum and natural gas are the most important ___ products. 2. In addition to petroleum and natural gas, some ___ products are gypsum, helium, limestone and salt.	**Mission(s)** 1. Reverend Isaac McCoy established a series of Baptist ___ throughout the new Indian Territory in 1830. 2. Dr. Lykins founded the Shawnee Baptist ___ near present-day Kansas City.
Missouri River 1. The ___ flows along the northeast border of the state. 2. The ___ is the longest river in North America.	**Motto** 1. The state ___ is *"Ad astra per aspera."* 2. In English the state ___ is "To the stars through difficulties."
Mount Sunflower 1. At 4,039 feet, ___ is the highest point in Kansas. 2. ___, the highest point in the state, is in the Great Plains near the Colorado border.	**Pawnee(s)** 1. There are four distinct bands of ___: Kitkahahki, Chaui, Petahauirata, and Skidi. The 4 bands are now recognized as one tribe. 2. The ___ lived in villages featuring dome-shaped earth lodges.
River(s) 1. The Arkansas, the Kansas, the Missouri, the Republican, and the Smoky Hill are ___ in Kansas. 2. The Kansas ___ is also known as the Kaw ___. Its name and nickname come from the Kanza, or Kaw, people who once inhabited the area. The state is named for the ___.	**Salamander** 1. The barred tiger ___ is the state amphibian. The juvenile larval stage is aquatic and has external gills. 2. The barred tiger ___ is mostly nocturnal. It lives near bodies of water where it can easily burrow into the soil.
Santa Fe Trail 1. This 19th-century route from Missouri to Santa Fe helped open the region to U.S. economic development and settlement. 2. The ___ crossed the territory of the Comanches, who demanded compensation for granting rights-of-way.	**Seal** 1. Commerce is represented on the Great ___ by a river and a steamboat. Agriculture is represented by a settler's cabin and a man plowing. 2. The 34 stars on the Great ___ identify Kansas as the 34th state to enter the Union.
Kansas Bingo	© **Barbara M. Peller**

Song

1. "Home on the Range" is the state ___.
2. The words to the state ___ were written by Dr. Brewster Higley. The music was written by words by Dan Kelly.

Southeastern Plains

1. The ___ can be divided into two sections: the Osage Plains and the Flint Hills.
2. Although both the ___ and the High Plains are a gently rolling landscape, the High Plains have a higher elevation.

Sunflower(s)

1. The wild native ___ is the state flower and floral emblem.
2. Kansas is known as the ___ State. Wild ___ grow in abundance across the state.

Topeka

1. ___ is the capital of Kansas and the county seat of Shawnee County.
2. ___ has been the capital since 1861.

Tornado (-oes)

1. A ___ is a violent rotating column of air. It is usually accompanied by a a funnel-shaped downward extension of a cumulonimbus cloud.
2. ___ occur when unstable hot air near the ground rises and meets the cooler air above in the thunder clouds.

Turtle

1. The ornate box ___ is the state reptile.
2. The ornate box ___ can completely withdraw its legs, tail, head and neck into its protective shell.

Tuttle Creek

1. ___ Reservoir was created by the Army Corps of Engineers for the purpose of flood control.
2. ___ Reservoir State Park is about 5 miles north of Manhattan.

Union

1. Kansas was admitted to the ___ as the 34th state on January 29, 1861.
2. On January 29, 1861, Kansas was admitted to the ___ as a free state.

Wheat

1. ___ is the state's largest crop. Corn for grain and soybeans are also valuable ___.
2. Kansas produces more ___ than any other state.

Wichita

1. ___ is located in south-central Kansas on the Arkansas River. It is the largest city in Kansas.
2. The Old Cowtown Museum in ___ lets visitors experience what it was like to live in the Old West.

Kansas Bingo

Kansas Bingo

Santa Fe Trail	Abilene	Amelia Mary Earhart	Indian Removal Act	Buffalo
Hard Chief's Village	Agricultural	Wheat	Mission(s)	Southeastern Plains
Union	Mined		High Plains	Wichita
Tuttle Creek	Song	Turtle	Meadowlark	Motto
Pawnee(s)	Kansas–Nebraska Act	Firefighter's Museum	Topeka	Little Bluestem

Kansas Bingo

Tuttle Creek	Union	Legislature	Seal	Louisiana Purchase
Motto	Flag	Crop(s)	Song	Mount Sunflower
Dodge City	Kansas–Nebraska Act		Leavenworth	Turtle
River(s)	Salamander	Mined	Lewis and Clark	Buffalo
Southeastern Plains	Wheat	Firefighter's Museum	Hard Chief's Village	Topeka

Kansas Bingo: Card No. 2

Kansas Bingo

Kansas–Nebraska Act	Turtle	Flag	Meadowlark	Union
Motto	Agricultural	Dissected Till Plains	Abilene	Kansas City
Song	Wheat		Mount Sunflower	Border
Mined	Dodge City	Pawnee(s)	River(s)	Legislature
Topeka	Earth Lodge(s)	Firefighter's Museum	Lewis and Clark	Louisiana Purchase

Kansas Bingo

Mined	Mount Sunflower	Amelia Mary Earhart	Earth Lodge(s)	Louisiana Purchase
Missouri River	County (-ies)	Abilene	Seal	Union
High Plains	River(s)		Little Bluestem	Indian Removal Act
Turtle	Agricultural	Wheat	Firefighter's Museum	Crop(s)
Dwight D. Eisenhower	Southeastern Plains	Chisholm Trail	Topeka	Wichita

Kansas Bingo

Southeastern Plains	Buffalo	Song	Crop(s)	Earth Lodge(s)
Missouri River	Turtle	Dissected Till Plains	Leavenworth	Agricultural
Amelia Mary Earhart	Wichita		Mission(s)	Judicial Branch
Little Bluestem	Louisiana Purchase	Santa Fe Trail	Lewis and Clark	Executive Branch
Flag	Firefighter's Museum	Union	Mined	High Plains

Kansas Bingo: Card No. 5

Kansas Bingo

Border	Mount Sunflower	Legislature	Louisiana Purchase	Wichita
Meadowlark	Song	Executive Branch	Abilene	Union
Seal	Dwight D. Eisenhower		County (-ies)	Leavenworth
Firefighter's Museum	Pawnee(s)	Lewis and Clark	Chisholm Trail	Amelia Mary Earhart
Motto	Crop(s)	Santa Fe Trail	High Plains	Harney Silt Loam

Kansas Bingo

Santa Fe Trail	Mount Sunflower	Judicial Branch	Turtle	Flag
Motto	Louisiana Purchase	Kansas–Nebraska Act	Agricultural	Missouri River
Wichita	Indian Removal Act		Leavenworth	County (-ies)
Mined	River(s)	Dissected Till Plains	Tuttle Creek	Dodge City
Firefighter's Museum	Earth Lodge(s)	Lewis and Clark	Chisholm Trail	Border

Kansas Bingo

High Plains	Mount Sunflower	Honeybee	Meadowlark	County (-ies)
Missouri River	Amelia Mary Earhart	Seal	Wichita	Crop(s)
Harney Silt Loam	Earth Lodge(s)		Louisiana Purchase	Buffalo
Topeka	Mined	Tuttle Creek	Dwight D. Eisenhower	River(s)
Wheat	Firefighter's Museum	Chisholm Trail	Song	Motto

Kansas Bingo

Leavenworth	Flag	Kansas–Nebraska Act	Harney Silt Loam	Earth Lodge(s)
Dwight D. Eisenhower	Louisiana Purchase	High Plains	Song	Mount Sunflower
Kansas City	Santa Fe Trail		Agricultural	Honeybee
Executive Branch	Buffalo	Pawnee(s)	Mission(s)	Judicial Branch
River(s)	Lewis and Clark	Dissected Till Plains	Tuttle Creek	Little Bluestem

Kansas Bingo: Card No. 9

Kansas Bingo

Tuttle Creek	Meadowlark	County (-ies)	Seal	Harney Silt Loam
Wichita	Crop(s)	Abilene	Agricultural	Louisiana Purchase
Earth Lodge(s)	Mount Sunflower		Indian Removal Act	Dodge City
Pawnee(s)	Little Bluestem	Executive Branch	Lewis and Clark	Kansas City
Dissected Till Plains	Motto	Legislature	Southeastern Plains	High Plains

Kansas Bingo: Card No. 10

Kansas Bingo

Border	Mount Sunflower	Song	Executive Branch	Motto
Honeybee	Kansas City	Mission(s)	Leavenworth	Abilene
Missouri River	Louisiana Purchase		Legislature	Kansas–Nebraska Act
Dissected Till Plains	Union	Lewis and Clark	Earth Lodge(s)	Tuttle Creek
Dwight D. Eisenhower	Firefighter's Museum	Santa Fe Trail	Chisholm Trail	Flag

Kansas Bingo

Flag	Buffalo	Kansas City	Meadowlark	Leavenworth
Kansas–Nebraska Act	Motto	Amelia Mary Earhart	Chisholm Trail	Agricultural
Santa Fe Trail	Judicial Branch		Wichita	Seal
Firefighter's Museum	River(s)	Louisiana Purchase	Tuttle Creek	Missouri River
Mount Sunflower	Honeybee	Earth Lodge(s)	Dwight D. Eisenhower	Crop(s)

Kansas Bingo

Executive Branch	Buffalo	Border	Kansas City	Wichita
Amelia Mary Earhart	Honeybee	Louisiana Purchase	Leavenworth	Dodge City
Meadowlark	Crop(s)		Kansas–Nebraska Act	Judicial Branch
High Plains	Lewis and Clark	County (-ies)	Earth Lodge(s)	Tuttle Creek
Firefighter's Museum	Little Bluestem	Chisholm Trail	Santa Fe Trail	Mission(s)

Kansas Bingo

Hard Chief's Village	Louisiana Purchase	Song	Leavenworth	Dwight D. Eisenhower
Crop(s)	Santa Fe Trail	Kansas City	Agricultural	Mount Sunflower
Executive Branch	Indian Removal Act		Legislature	Dissected Till Plains
Little Bluestem	Lewis and Clark	Earth Lodge(s)	County (-ies)	Border
Firefighter's Museum	Seal	Dodge City	Motto	High Plains

Kansas Bingo: Card No. 14

Kansas Bingo

Mission(s)	Leavenworth	Song	Flag	Meadowlark
Border	Legislature	Abilene	Amelia Mary Earhart	Dwight D. Eisenhower
Wichita	Santa Fe Trail		Union	Mount Sunflower
Firefighter's Museum	Kansas City	Honeybee	Lewis and Clark	Executive Branch
Motto	River(s)	Chisholm Trail	Harney Silt Loam	Kansas–Nebraska Act

Kansas Bingo

County (-ies)	Kansas City	Honeybee	Harney Silt Loam	Salamander
Seal	Dodge City	Judicial Branch	Missouri River	Indian Removal Act
Executive Branch	Buffalo		Wichita	Kansas–Nebraska Act
Mined	Crop(s)	Firefighter's Museum	Mission(s)	Tuttle Creek
Dwight D. Eisenhower	Tornado (-oes)	Chisholm Trail	River(s)	Mount Sunflower

Kansas Bingo: Card No. 16

Kansas Bingo

Dissected Till Plains	Sunflower(s)	Little Raven	Kansas City	Hard Chief's Village
Mission(s)	Dwight D. Eisenhower	Lewis and Clark	Indian Removal Act	Judicial Branch
Leavenworth	High Plains		Tornado (-oes)	Honeybee
Little Bluestem	Motto	Tuttle Creek	Song	Dodge City
Pawnee(s)	Executive Branch	Flag	Meadowlark	Buffalo

Kansas Bingo

Harney Silt Loam	Earth Lodge(s)	Crop(s)	Executive Branch	Seal
Mount Sunflower	Dissected Till Plains	Pawnee(s)	Wichita	Dwight D. Eisenhower
Leavenworth	Dodge City		Little Raven	Amelia Mary Earhart
Buffalo	Abilene	Lewis and Clark	Tuttle Creek	Legislature
Tornado (-oes)	Kansas City	Song	Sunflower(s)	Border

Kansas Bingo: Card No. 18

© Barbara M. Peller

Kansas Bingo

Wichita	Border	Kansas City	Honeybee	Tuttle Creek
Mission(s)	Meadowlark	Mount Sunflower	Flag	Indian Removal Act
Sunflower(s)	Earth Lodge(s)		Agricultural	Union
Legislature	Tornado (-oes)	Pawnee(s)	River(s)	Little Raven
Amelia Mary Earhart	Salamander	Motto	High Plains	Chisholm Trail

Kansas Bingo

Hard Chief's Village	Sunflower(s)	Meadowlark	Kansas City	Chisholm Trail
Crop(s)	Kansas–Nebraska Act	Missouri River	Pawnee(s)	Seal
Buffalo	Judicial Branch		Mined	Abilene
Southeastern Plains	Wheat	Topeka	River(s)	Tornado (-oes)
Turtle	High Plains	Salamander	Tuttle Creek	Little Raven

Kansas Bingo

Mission(s)	Border	Missouri River	Kansas City	Southeastern Plains
Buffalo	Little Raven	County (-ies)	Honeybee	Santa Fe Trail
Dodge City	Motto		Sunflower(s)	Song
Pawnee(s)	Flag	Tornado (-oes)	Little Bluestem	High Plains
Mined	Salamander	Chisholm Trail	Dissected Till Plains	River(s)

Kansas Bingo

Harney Silt Loam	Legislature	Little Raven	Amelia Mary Earhart	Executive Branch
Seal	Meadowlark	Union	Honeybee	Agricultural
Crop(s)	Indian Removal Act		Santa Fe Trail	Judicial Branch
Tornado (-oes)	Little Bluestem	River(s)	Abilene	Missouri River
Salamander	Dissected Till Plains	Sunflower(s)	Dodge City	Mined

Kansas Bingo

County (-ies)	Sunflower(s)	Flag	Amelia Mary Earhart	Chisholm Trail
Border	Hard Chief's Village	Motto	Mission(s)	Abilene
Legislature	Executive Branch		Topeka	Santa Fe Trail
Dodge City	Salamander	Tornado (-oes)	Dissected Till Plains	River(s)
Southeastern Plains	Wheat	High Plains	Pawnee(s)	Little Raven

Chisholm Trail	Amelia Mary Earhart	Flag	Sunflower(s)	County(-ies)

Kansas Bingo

County (-ies)	High Plains	Hard Chief's Village	Sunflower(s)	Honeybee
Little Raven	Chisholm Trail	Missouri River	Seal	Santa Fe Trail
Judicial Branch	Harney Silt Loam		Executive Branch	Dodge City
Southeastern Plains	Topeka	Tornado (-oes)	Dissected Till Plains	Buffalo
Turtle	Mined	Salamander	Meadowlark	Wheat

Kansas Bingo

Mined	Missouri River	Sunflower(s)	Song	Little Raven
Abilene	Buffalo	Mission(s)	County (-ies)	Agricultural
Little Bluestem	Honeybee		Topeka	Tornado (-oes)
Union	Southeastern Plains	Wheat	Salamander	Indian Removal Act
Chisholm Trail	Hard Chief's Village	Crop(s)	Dwight D. Eisenhower	Turtle

Kansas Bingo: Card No. 25

Kansas Bingo

Little Raven	Sunflower(s)	Legislature	Seal	Harney Silt Loam
Pawnee(s)	Meadowlark	Honeybee	Hard Chief's Village	County (-ies)
Little Bluestem	Topeka		Indian Removal Act	Mined
Dissected Till Plains	Amelia Mary Earhart	Southeastern Plains	Salamander	Tornado (-oes)
Judicial Branch	Dwight D. Eisenhower	Song	Wheat	Turtle

Kansas Bingo

Legislature	Crop(s)	Sunflower(s)	Hard Chief's Village	Kansas–Nebraska Act
Southeastern Plains	Topeka	Mission(s)	Tornado (-oes)	Agricultural
Lewis and Clark	Wheat		Salamander	Mined
Harney Silt Loam	Border	Missouri River	Turtle	Abilene
Dwight D. Eisenhower	Indian Removal Act	Little Raven	Union	Judicial Branch

Kansas Bingo

Legislature	Hard Chief's Village	Union	Sunflower(s)	County (-ies)
Kansas–Nebraska Act	Little Raven	Topeka	Seal	Indian Removal Act
Wheat	Dodge City		Judicial Branch	Pawnee(s)
Tuttle Creek	Harney Silt Loam	Motto	Salamander	Tornado (-oes)
Amelia Mary Earhart	Leavenworth	Dwight D. Eisenhower	Turtle	Southeastern Plains

Kansas Bingo

Little Raven	Hard Chief's Village	Harney Silt Loam	Mission(s)	Leavenworth
River(s)	Pawnee(s)	Missouri River	Judicial Branch	Union
Little Bluestem	Topeka		Agricultural	Sunflower(s)
Kansas–Nebraska Act	Southeastern Plains	Louisiana Purchase	Salamander	Tornado (-oes)
County (-ies)	Honeybee	Turtle	Border	Wheat

Kansas Bingo

Earth Lodge(s)	Sunflower(s)	Seal	Leavenworth	Tornado (-oes)
Abilene	Hard Chief's Village	Legislature	Indian Removal Act	Agricultural
Little Bluestem	Executive Branch		Judicial Branch	Missouri River
Turtle	Border	Amelia Mary Earhart	Salamander	Topeka
Southeastern Plains	Wichita	Wheat	Little Raven	Union

Kansas Bingo: Card No. 30